# From Concentrate

# From Concentrate

### Poems by

### K.E. Robiscoe

Cover design by Shay Culligan
Cover art by lolloj

ISBN: 978-1-952326-84-4

Kelsay Books
502 South 1040 East, A-119
American Fork, Utah, 84003

For James Robert Fletcher

—without whom none of me would

have been possible—

# Acknowledgments

*The Raven Journal:* "Poe-Po' Polly"

*The Moon Magazine:* "Rain-catcher"

*300 Days of Sun, Issue #3:* "Addiction," "Schaden-Freud"

*Broken City; Remotely Controlled:* "3 Hour Tour"

*Lunch Ticket, Issue #8:* "Violet Rain"

*Sand Canyon Review; 2015 publication:* "wUnderLand"

*Main Street Rag:* "Talking Shop"

*Silver Birch Press:* "With Sugar on Top"

*Midnight Circus Volume #8:* "Piecemeal Photosynthesis," "Home-nyms"

*Gangleri's Grove:* "Ferry Tale Endings"

*Steam Ticket; A Third Coast Review:* "Good Penny"

*Spectrum Anthology at UCSB, # CLVV:* "New Shoes"

*Spectrum Anthology at UCSB, # CLVIV:* "The Write Ingredients"

*Handful of Dust:* "Wash Day"

*Word Mosaics:* "Pie-Pie Blackbird," "Daisy Bouquet," "For Cloudless Times," "Homophone Cookin'," "Graceland," "Monday thru Friday"

# Contents

# …and the Kitchen Sync

He is Georgia
(on my mind)
*the one near Russia*
dba Graceland,
*the tourist attraction Graceland*
He is the Mississippi,
*log-jammed*
West Virginia
*rocky mountain to scale*
and hey, I'm a globe trotter—
he's England & Paris, too,
*run riot*
He is the desert
*and the reason the desert exists*
and the See
*a big splash*
the stars
*the asterisks kind*
and the sun
*and everything under it…*
the mUse
*reams of parchment*
and the music
*sorry, Casey!*
He is the rapids of Crazy River
upstream
*black water.*

# Shore-break

She waded at a silent shore,
testing brink of now & then
—and whispered wish for sands before

and missing him a life or more
sought the shoals of why & when,
She waded at a silent shore

as sirens will a sea implore,
on weighted buoy of hope & yen
—and whispered wish for sands before

that any tide, or swearing for
could not undo, nor change amend,
She waded at a silent shore

impelled to seek by deepest core,
confusing, fixed phenomenon
—and whispered wish for sands before

for beacon lost atop *a moor*
that trumped all start & stayed all end
She waded at a silent shore
—and whispered wish for sands before…

# …don't forget the…

*Freezer Aisle*
heart
(remember to defrost!)

*Snacks:*
~~Eye Candy~~
Sugar

*Entertainment:*
(Doh! left that outdoors!)

*Household Supplies:*
Unconditional Love
Time

*Hardware:*
um…

*Staples:*
WD elbow grease

*Produce:*
Content

# Helen's Song

against melted sherbet sky,
and crumbling breakwater
a gridiron gull perched—

—faceted in prism, and
arcing rainbows that
ache into saltwater—

impervious to the break of
Sentient Sentences,
etching brackish reverse in swan feet

—spilling the Grit of Ages to wind.

since love is a compound wound.
a contrary homeostasis.
its Form relevant only by occasion.

So you see, Sweet Paris…
Nothing's changed…
You've only just now noticed

—the tattoo—

pounding heart
of electric wave
finding *eternal* shores

until even Poseidon breathes fire

# Helen's Lament

And now I am lost
Paris,
your sensibilities leave me
—I perish...

A sun's brilliance
distant, behind horizon
a world far
—relinquished.

To Wall, War, and Veil
careening galaxies away
solar storm
—finished,

unheeded burn and beckon
agents orange
against black-edged print
—rubbish…

a Milky Way imitation
where sweeping steps boast
unmet landings
—I languish

obscured in mushroom mist
—all cherished—
implodes and expands

…unending…
…unexpended…

# Silent Stadium

For the fourth place winner
there is no fanfare,
no spot on a dais,
nor humble expression required...
Fourth place—in itself—is already humility.

There will be no need
for the fourth place winner to attend
the celebratory dinner,
no need to prepare a speech,
thanking Mom and Dad, and possibly
a surprise figure from his past.

Mom and Dad are secretly embarrassed
—for all that they say otherwise—

since the fourth place winner
should understand
*now*
(instead of later)
that there *is* no fourth place.

Not really...
not in actual sporting events,
and not in life, and
this rectangle of
criss-cut satin yellow
is panacea,
is the "no booing" rule
ramped up a notch,
is an eye-patch waiting to happen—

a fourth place loser
that Nobody applauds
—not really—
Nobody is rooting for the winner!
(along with Everybody Else)

who is always
three steps ahead—

# Poe-Po' Polly

It was the witchin' hour,
a power tower glitchin' hour,
a black as hell & bitchin' hour,
in every sense of word.
Because a bit contrarily,
and yes, a trifle wearily,
I'm here to tell you verily,
the word is *not* the bird.

The bird in fact, is wordy
—for all that he's a birdee
and though it sounds absurd he—
roosts with boys in blue.
And sure as bells are knellin',
come midnight he's a yellin',
puttin' me through hell an',
gettin' all gumshoe.

He cackles and he coos,
and parrot-izes news, and
asks me: where were you?
(and then he spews some more)
Rhetoric embracin'—
some repeated phrases,
people, things, and places,
includin' poor Lenore.

A chick who I found sexy
(at least until she left me)
sayin' it was best, we—
seek a separate road.
Didn't learn 'til later,
she vanished at equator,
just assumed she made her-
-self a new abode.

Now worse than AWOL mistress,
is I'm a peep of interest
(birdee's here on business)
raptor-captor style.
Searchin' through my mansion…
Perchin' on my transom…
and though I offered ransom—
he's stayin' 'til the trial.

# Pie-Pie Blackbird

The raven was dour
the hour was late,
his feed cup was empty
and so was his plate,
and since he liked talking
(aka) bitching
he crowed out his anger
to folks in the kitchen.

He cackled injustice
He cawed of: "starvation!"
He made a huge ruckus
for MIA rations,
then poked at
the eyeballs—
of resident cook,
a poor choice
since that was
the last peck he took.

As near blinded Cookie
made snap decisions—
and spurred by the damage
done to his vision,
grabbed up the Raven
by leathery talon,
sealed him in pastry
and turned up the oven,

and though Cookie thought
his answer was cunning,
the Raven was given
to afternoon sunning,
and later that evening
when pie was removed,
he popped from the top
and cawed:

"No way dude!"

# s'Miley Poem

in Frosted wood
a Poe-sy could
Walt at time of pickin'...

but sharp Whitman
will bring a can
of water for that Dickens…

# Rain-catcher

He was a wayfaring
work of peace,
a wind traveler
—alone
(save a dog that glowed)
and bottles brimming with Soul, man
~and some accumulated fluff~
he was tender of spirits
—flasks filled with
rain, and
tied to his belt with bows—
—bows gathered from foggy frontlines,
and a different draft to war
—he wore flasks.

Cruets—
he had
cruets.
Charmed arm bands
dripping with
tears, and stopped
(at the top)
with heart—
—hearts pinned with arrows, and
broken
(though loosed) with
Eros intent
lacking insight
—he had cruets.

Decanters of dreams—
(and some canteens)
in haversack, he carried
decanters of breathless dreams…

Darkest dreams caught by
feathered hawk
~wing without weave~
and moon missing shadow—
—he carried dreams…

Skipping stone
(and ritual)
at water's edge,
when he spoke
—rarely, since he was missing—
he sang.

# Addiction

I am addiction
I
Am bigger than you
I
Am better than you
I
Am more *you* than you
will ever be and
I
get angry if you stop.


I won't stop until I stop you completely.


Nothing matters more than me
I
Am not dead—not dormant—not controlled
I
laugh at your good intentions
I
diminish your will
I
show you who's who
I
show you what's what


I show you, you are nothing compared to me.

I own you
I
won't release you
I
eat you alive as
I
prey for your death—


and then
I move on.

# Schaden-Freud

ID eat a horse
—if horse were
*fair*—
just for 1<sup>st</sup> course
if it were there…

ID sleep for days
—if
*daze*
were free—
existin' dream
between the "be"…

ID smoke a bale
—if
*bail*
were small—
just tellin' tales
short & Tall…

ID buy a mallet
—for the *maul*
ID spree—
to phallic
peen & ball…

My Super Ego's
—half ID's size
ID over dues—
all lows & highs.

# 3 Hour Tour

I stowed away
with castaways,
got lost for days
just floatin',
drifted to
a green lagoon,
on pontoon
saved from boatin',

built some huts
with bamboo struts.
with coconuts
for shingles,
caught a sow
for dinner chow
and held luau
to mingle,

of ladies three
the pedigree
the richest she
was older,
while hourglass
defined the lass
(the tits and ass)
that smoldered,
the girl next door
in shorty shorts
she wore

her tresses plaited,
baked some pies
to please the guys
—a partner shy
of dating,
(a walking check)
(an intellect)
(the boss of wreck)
(and matey)

since hull was toast
we lived on coast
composing SOS's,
the theme of show
for year or mo'
but which show,
can you guess it?

# Violet Rain

two months at best
the doc said,
and we went home…
—in drowning rain
—in pregnant silence
—in circular, useless thought

* houseplants *
* houseplants *
* houseplants *

(need watering)

and we're still out of milk…
'better remember to—
oh!
a new lymphatic system!
you need
a new lymphatic system, too…

'missing red lights
that beamed like
land bound sentinels
worn-out
windshield wipers
smearing grey horizon
over everything
.choking view.

obscuring doorways
faceting teardrops
blurring petals
of withered African violet
(the one in the foyer)
(the one that's been there as long as I've known you)
(the one that needed watering sooner)

leaves falling
like fuzzy rain…

like two months left
to live
(at best)

# Daisy Bouquet

*Party of One*
*your table is ready*
the Sudden Maître de announces
(from behind left shoulder)
and though One has reservations
* Maître D' doesn't *
and so One goes…


The place is trimmed in satin
(as if for a VIP)
Black tie required, though Maître D' wears a hoodie
—padded and bowed—
since despite the bad neighborhood
simply every One lingers
—even Americans!
dead ringer cord available upon request
(the last)


*There's an*
*eco-friendly special*
the Grim Maître D' says, shoving One hard into place.
*an all-natural preparation*
(no MSG)
*new and dated all at once*
(no Styrofoam)
*since the "to go" bag is meant to spoil*
*and may, in fact, be seeded.*

*If all that fails to tempt*
*Chef will make an exception*
the Grim Maître D' ends, snapping finger-bones restlessly.

will in fact, prepare a custom order
(rare)
Providing One brought a Dash
—a medium—
and doesn't mind the heat.
(well done)

# an uneXpected Dash

When people you love die,
they move from rooms—
to the *walls* of rooms…
* 90 degree angle *
that alchemically flattens Life.


Jack-knifing the form out of them,
the life and warm out of them,
the strife and norm out of them—
that last a universally shared projection.


When people you love die,
their effects move from *their* rooms—
to boxes and furniture in *your* rooms…
* cardboard containers *
that definitively reduces Life.


Residual vase to
grace considered place
—to vestigially trace—
that first a universally shared necessity.


When people you love die,
they move to the room past being,
to the room the being *cannot* pass…
* transmuted energy *
of eternally altered Life.

The where of them a wish, now—
Shared journey at its finish, now—
Their burdens so relinquished, now—
that between a universally shared blessing.

# Baby Blue

He wore blue on Mondays
~sky-blue~
and so regularly, too,
you could set your clock by it,
and maybe the sun did—
—since it was always sunny when you were with Baby Blue.

On Wednesday, he wore grey
Baby Blue outfit in need of laundering, now,
laundering that somehow fell behind
depleting water unremarked…
extra scoops of
poppy-scented detergent added—
—detergent so strong it near washed Baby Blue away along with it,
and maybe it did.
since the sky was suddenly grey that day at Baby Blue's

By Friday, Baby Blue wore Black.
*for the first time*
Horribly slimming it was, too,
*for the last time*
but stylish teak hampers brimmed
with charred bits of Baby Blue
*bye then*
sealed with hella strong Krazy Glue, and
not even a handful of ashes scattered to the wind, and
six feet is a long way to dig for freedom, and
shouting
—though helpful—
won't get that grass stain out…

I'm sure that it won't.
Not when nightfall eclipses afternoon sky
and arrives
without twilight.

# wUndergroUnd

hare sniPPers
lop off ears
stick Van Goghs
to Walls & shear
making Hatter's
stovepipe chic
~safety gear~
haz-mat geek
but tardy rabbit
shorn
of sound
wanders
'round
in Wonder Town
recallin' when the
Rabbit Hole
was
halcyon
for Hares
on go.

# Talking Shop

I take out my words
and buff them
*—often—*
Like a mechanic, I tinker
adjusting the suspension,
checking the
.brakes.
Watching my reflection in
the chrome all the while.

Peddling my mettle
with detail and regret,
I strip and embellish.
Tightening nuts
and loosening gears,
discarding custom parts
*—as needed—*
And backseat drivers, too.

I dry spit
& polish rhetoric.
Plugging sparks, and
tuning up timing belts.
Greasing a few poems
along the way, I
*—wax on and on and—*
(wraparound light poles)

Rebuilding idioms
—*to my own aesthetic*—
I thumb rides to move forward,
and clutch at inspiration.
Sure, I blow out at high speeds,
but I get wicked good mileage,
and if I run out of drive,
There's always cruise control.

# With Sugar on Top

Summer came, and
enthralled by dopplering music emanating
from that cool truck
*—Van Halen, naturally—*
Dairy Queen
chased Good Humor
down a Rocky Road…

loose stones
> thrown >
*and waffling cones*
—creating a Ripple effect in pooled cream—
Wavy Gravy sped toward
Sunday's edge

*the jimmies gone, the whip dissolved*

discovering
en Rooty
the world was *indeed* round,
there *was* such a thing
as Tooty
(much)
topping
(nuts, 2)
and glass was *house,* not Brickle…

Butter scoop a Truffle
too late
to re·verse sweet tsunami
*contain* her!
but not Mud Pies.

41

# Cake's Boss

affection confection
is kindness that's rindless
) (
its sweet pip,
a cream dip,
& cherry whip,
minus—
pits, stops, & lashes,
unless maso-
-kisstic
sadistically
chissing
deep down in the mYstic
bonding like batter
that's spicy
&
~rising~
a marzipan phatter,
than moJo surprising—
—than
ticklish
licker-ish,
a
sweet·tart·the·tang
is huggable drug—
(( ))
& heady meringue.

# Batter Apart

Cookie & Breadstick got together
*at start and stop dinner*
and lived well-off Divinity for a while
*it's very rich*
and everything else crumby until
things got stale,
and Breadstick went to hell…

*he needed the heat to stay hard*

Cookie getting all Betty Crocker with a need to conform…
*became a secret Cutter*
who never dared use
Sprinkles,
or Icing,
or even Powdered Sugar,
without Stick's go ahead, who
mean·time
morphed into the Doughboy…

Burying Pil's in his breadbasket to get through dinner,
while Cookie Cutter hit the sauce pretty hard,
mixed up rum balls
(to cover)
*burnt Pan several times in the process*
—and most associated utensils—
and it was inevitable that both glutens eventually batched out…

Retiring to the shelves of the Big 4 store from which Breadstick
and Cookie hailed, to await the return to
the Baker
—the *real* Baker—
all sixes & sevens & sum
13.

# Piecemeal Photosynthesis

My written leaves
mulch soil…

soil bought at
"Home Depot", and together
you and I
foster a nascent sappy tree.
(a tree without pith)

ostensibly devoted to class order
—and family ancestry.
To parallel future
—and wishful thinking.
(an emotional weave more fragile than Dandelion Fuzz)

these cyber shrines
lend the impression
of forrested terrain…

Tunguskan
by virtue of…
Make-up?
Annihilation?
Chance?
—it's hard to say…
Hard to see, really—
what with all those trees.

DPI or defined—
trees can't suck lemons
(not even lemon trees!)
and they don't lick salt,
(or suffer its rub in knotholes)
And they absolutely refuse

to piece together
tequila nights
bit by blacked-out bit,
splicing maybe into faqs
rendering them phantoms—all.
(despite the heavy thicket)

And now estranged, I graft remnants of excess into ghosts,
(the ones mandated to play dress-up)
Imagining the day you'll like me better…
the day you'll upload pictures of *me*
with clever and informational captions
creating an album
only strangers view.

# For Cloudless Times

I took a picture of a cloud
with my arm...
Uploaded it to a cloud
with my arm...

So the next time it was sunny
—and I was *not*—
there would be clouds
within arms reach.

# Projections

so this is how it is:
you go for a walk
—*a run, if you can*—
and
the Fed-ex truck drives by,
and you go to wave automatic-like
mouth turning up at the edges, already,
then you remember Leo don't
drive it no more
—*energy pushing outward unmet*—
Leo died from
the Cancer
a few months back, and so young, too
—*not that young, twelve years older or so*—
and your hand drops
—*unexpressed*—
and it's a little thing, really, but it's a *thing,* all right,
a minus where there used to be a plus.

then the mail guy comes
but it ain't Big John driving USPS snail or shine
—*smart John, too*—
for all his wooly whiskers
and gin blossom cheeks
Big John could talk circles around
the Literature,
—*sweet John*—
but Big John died, too, or maybe he retired, but Big John ain't
the mail person no more
—*and who cares? it's just mail, but you do a little*—
(a lot)
*and it adds to the thing that subtracts.*

so you go to the café for some coffee
—*for company*—
the café that hangs all the pictures of the locals
on the walls, and
all your friends, too,
but they don't do that no more, neither,
—*the friends you had MIA*—
the spot where
your picture hung
is empty, now
—*and maybe you are, too, a little*—

a faded square of wallpaper the only
reminder
this used to be
your place.

# Desperately Seeking Tom Robbins

I moved to Hidden Valley—
since life became distressing…
on the table,
on the label,
under words that spell: Ranch-Dressing.

The fields are ripe for harvest,
the planted rows are green—
—and veggies are
like candy bars!
And everything's so clean.

The people there are sparkling!
their *joie de vivre* plain…
the ice cream treats,
are made from beets,
the kind that *never* stain.

The sky is always sunny—
the clouds just fluffy balls.
the only rain,
organic grain,
no GMO's at all.

Maybe come tomorrow,
I'll hike toward bright horizon,
follow sun—
—when salad's done
see what's behind the hyphen.

# Home-nyms

would Fil agree
to columns
or would he glaze the roof
would eaves then drop
would knockers knock
would steps refuse to stoop?

would par•a•pets
go missing...
to portico by two's
would rams then part
for Hall on Arch
and drift to Bay with view?

if wooden boats
are houses
and houses wooden boats…
why not museum
or coliseum
afloat with gilded goats?

# Homophone Cookin'

I cook tales with too much metaphor
dredge words in too much flower,
Mix truth with lies and super-size
abstractions sweet and sour.

I double-boil mysteries
and reduce the residue,
'Til whodunits are a pasty fend
of well-done "it", and "who".

I tenderize my poetry
that simmers day and night,
In great quatrains of thyme-less broth
Until the bites are write.

For dessert I like a simile
served hot and à lle gory,
Steep leaves of me in imagery
and belch a finished story.

# Kan-do

we're all so fully fallible—
our foibles→refillable
> inborn & instill-able <
—accept it
—to the syl•la•ble—
Enjoy it!
Make it
*$ billable $*
As facades
> though employable <
are fables for the
~flappable~
both sappy &
/ implacable /
a go-to for the
p l i a b l e
a fallback
that's detestable
*unviable & liable*
to render tender
* jest-able *
as bending truth is
^ laughable ^
& also Google trackable
exposing like Pinocchio
a posing braggadocio
a—nose—so—long→
it's joke—
—ay?

Yo!

(deep breath)

…while frontages more facile…
Will prove that you're no asshole.

# Ferry Tale Endings

Charon's Ferry
(bait and tackle)
set up shop near River Styx,
at its nexus
south of Texas
selling river-crossing trips,
the only charge
to ride that barge
a coin between your lips
assuming death
has stopped your breath
when booking you on ship….

& once aboard
with demon horde
you'll find there's much to do,
since power boats
don't cross the moat
between Abyss and you,
> at very least <
that Charon beast
expects you work the crew,
so bring a paddle
like rest of chattel
'fore jumpin' on canoe.

Then feel free
(the last you'll be)
to look around the lake,
some residents
¡were presidents!
but there's no Watergate—
—no Hoover dam
but Dick's herb and
that's mood Depressing shake
(Herb shovels sh*t
around the Pit
with pointless, taxing rakes)

There's Bordens, too
and Gorgons, who
are not as stoned as last time,
it's best to peek
with glance oblique
since stoning is their pastime,
avoiding stares
(& whispered prayers)
should save you from that cast eye
a payoff huge
since Pan will use
your stones for breaking glass shrines...

But when you dock
across the Loch
make sure your hands aren't idle,
as Devil loves
his ownsome gloves

not yours—that sh*t's just libel
assist offload
as if you're Job
both actual, and Bible,
secure the gang-
-way, try to hang
way back in case of tidal
↓ ebb & flow ↑
of flames can throw
you face to face with idols.

—a closing tip—
there's no round trip,
your destination's final.

# Good Penny

I'll love you if, I'll love you when
my heart remembers beating
until before, forever friend

the never was & was that's been
will bear no more repeating
I'll love you if, I'll love you when

the lure of lore & anxious ken
no longer finds me bleeding
until before, forever friend

the light of you begetting yen
that distance failed defeating
I'll love you if, I'll love you when

the fear is gone, by deed & pen
—eternity is fleeting—
until before, forever friend

exceeding measure known to men
all fatuous competing
I'll love you if, I'll love you when
until before, forever friend.

# Graceland

Let's sit in black velvet, Elvis,
under a jawbreaker moon.

Expect a firmament
dripping sugar crystal
—clear and blue floss
just at sundown, streaking
stadium-sized meteors
that tat wholes
—out of holes—

shaping ephemeral
auroras into
(Western Nights)

Saltwater taffy our jammed Tootsies
Popped into shore-breaking
—with laughter
an unguarded medicine—

rolling & cresting whatever
ails you
…
if anything does
—ease it for you.

Let's do that…
you & me
…
sometime.

# Monday thru Friday

Rainy Monday crushed on TGF
(That Girl Friday)
poured get up and go,
cats and dogs,
and sodden checks, too,
into the second day…
(a delightful afternoon)
but log-jammed on Wednesday's grade.
'Bristled lightning at the delay
struck hammer blows—
in thunderous, 24/7 drumroll
and Tapped out at sunrise…
(the beginning of the best)
the dawn of indulgence,
a payday unspoken for
and no real rules at all.

In this oasis of
pivotal construct,
Monday and Friday
>merged<
living a life of Saturdays,
that slept an extra hour…
'Spilled coffee on rumpled sheets,
and crafted reel-to-real memories,
(with glitter and Elmer's Glue)
'Spooned weekend-flavored ice-cream
into bottomless bowls,
* erasing headlines *
and red-penning subterfuge…

incidentally creating
a human interest story
that could run
all week.

# New Shoes

I am a snake-eyed chef,
a boxcar attendant—afraid
The pendulum of doom swings in our direction.
Like so many of the masses.


I expect the sucker punch,
the unsolicited slap,
So surprising—still
The blow from behind.


Accurately sudden sweep,
Sweat stink-ridden grip to the next,
Careless Hand of space and time,
Only the divine sends us smothering into fetid darkness.


"Kiss it baby, for luck"


Crushing pressure,
Thrown at the wall of predictable fate,
to change each other—
or copy one another.


Surrendering
to an unknowable quantity,
Vital to believe—
Emerging unexpectedly high an—

Eleven on a scale of twelve,
a talented chance to change, and I
Leave the table as one.
Cash in my chips to buy—


The right to a
New and undefined
Me—I can't wait
to break the box.

# The Write Ingredients

I seasoned my work—an I amb stew,
with a measure of memory; added two
leaves of Bay that swooned, and cried—
to melt inside
my roiling page.

Wrote leaves of Sage to follow,
Its Self-Important Syllables
Too Savory to Swallow
in one gulp
so I ground them into pulp
—Chapters.
Diced tender shoots of Time and
threw basted dreams in
—after
a sprinkling of rhymes.

Shook similes and tried it,
tossed images inside it
Added more
metaphors,
…and a dash of…
… hesitation…
…' four afterthoughts went
streaming in
my steaming combination,

I turned it down to low, and next
Stirred and Stirred and left my text
as is typically my style.
Dreamt something else a little while.

But when the odor grew too strong
I was lured before too long
to whisk and sift, my well-done word,
And while It seemed to be
Overdone In Spots, to me
Absurd
with *Purple Prose,*
—and a trace too much erase—
Overall the things I chose
Tasted right in place.
Put a smile on my face.
And it thrilled with its frilled bones.

The seared slab of life my own
Truth, topped with my bundle of say—
My Book garni,
an elegant finish
to enhance
an Aged Soul.
And since my wit had simmered and mellowed for so
Many years
I served it up,
Immediately.

In dishes edged in gold
Full of my tale untold
Delicate menus in flowing script
tucked into napkins there,
inviting You to Dinner
with a
Place Card
at each chair.

# The First Housewarming Party

You'll notice
we're nudists—
no clothing on
boot-es—
no clothes
in abode-us
> it's just not our modus <
no clothing about us
we just do without it
* no fig leaf between us *
(you might see a penis)
some nattily matted,
but visible pubis
(it isn't a Rubiks)
God isn't a cubist
—nor nit-picking Goddess
in ripped-to-nip bodice...
Nor, too, for that matter
a true absolutist,
No, net of this ode is
religious
—but prude-es...

the nut
covered up
all props to the fruit-us.

# One Enchanted Evening

At loose ends,
God fashioned Adam
first of Men,
from über Dad
and finding gaps,
then added Madam

—*Brink of Night* He carved from Rib,
giving her a whittled fig'
an "hour-glassy" scrimshaw chick…

Despite the ***paring***—
—Madam grappled,
(hidden urges)
~~banned in chapel~~
& after sharing
♣ Adam's Apple ♣,
ditched his Pip to kiss a Toad,
—who as most know from lore of old,
can alter Toad's genetic code…

Since well-disguised
• by warty outers •
resided prince with
~ morphing power ~
trumping Airs
of diner dour
—whose tabled manners lacked noblesse—
needed breeding and finesse,
a want for which she sought redress,

to move as **maid**
from biased Garden,
to flyest pad & lily pardons,
where dual acts are not regarded,
with views unkind & spirits hardened—
—and thus when Madam
> made from ribs <
kissed her Adam's
nemesis
it made Dam glad that this exhibit,
did in no way Adam
mimic,
a truer *pairing*—
almost mythic!

—was
♠ Eve of Night ♠
&
♥ Prince from Ribbit ♥

# Original Spread

Add-man,
and right away
he has a hankering for Ribs.

Enter Even.
*someone's* got to cook, and
Odds are, the fruit plate will
excite goose-bumps
—starting a Side of Venom
followed by spot-on desserts

*> I'm lying—it's just more fruit <*

dress codes,
and the first argument ever
over "who ordered what"
Delivery and take-out only—
—Garden seating is booked.

# Wash Day

I'm painting a mural of another world
on my laundry room door
(closet, really)
So that washing clothes will be more
than a cycle of set-in stains

Basket on hip, the door will open to a wondrous place—
the common deep inside unique…
that spins into space
soaked in mystery, and peppered with white lights
brighter than bleach

I will reach for peace and fabric softener sheets
(mindful) yet mind-free in
this montage of remembered green
measure gritted hope against dewy sweat
that never made it into the hamper

I'm painting a mural of another world
on my laundry room door
(closet, really)
so the task matches the infinite more
—found in the seams of dreams.

# War-Drobe

Linked bracelets keep arms from flying,
and money-colored nails crucify palms in pointed, pointless
stigmata
Curb but create a fisting problem, along with
matching ring cuffs which
Eyeballed size is so off eventual amputation
is a shoo in,
and ultimate, future ice-breaker, besides.

as in: "nice nubs—is that hereditary?"

Belt skips leg-up loops,
but bands gut feeling
(more effective than surgery for wait control)
while thinking caps damn overflowing brains
though some synapses spill out that little flap in the back,
anyway…
That flap that gives way altogether on the swelled heads lockering
average minds
releasing collateral mediocrity into the atmosphere like so many
GHG's.

Jackrabbit feet
> start <
> stop <
> start <
> stop <
(start and stop, and start and stop, and start and stop, and so on—
losing any sincere punctuation along the way)

*held back))))*

by broken streetlights,
and sock puppet races.
By tightly-laced shoes,
and missing bootstraps,
By sick sense
and experience,
and to top that—necklaces!
Necklaces of all things,
you wouldn't think…

Well, necklaces…
Made of chain they leash,
and silk can loop & lynch,
since it's probably adulterated, you know.
A pilling, power cord
of Unplugged boundary
that loosens by the 2$^{nd}$
but chokes a 1$^{st}$ rate, Winchester noose for most everyone at least
once.
(I'd hazard to say)

Slung in secret over dissolving moonbeams
just persistent enough to last
until tags pop off heifer-pierced ears…
Until cheeks full of tongue darts explode!

# Hard Soap—Soft Water

at day's end, I
ablute—like any good girl, I

remove,

rinsing my eyes
with glue
> a staple <
to fix the tearing problem I've developed, I

wipe away.

washing mud, smoke, and stars from them
with full-grown oil,
*cracking kaleidoscope lens, I*

replace.

brushing my tongue with soap
*lye soap*
to tone down the acid situation there
that's a step away from vulgarity, a chronic condition my dentist
can't fix
*linguist either, I*

garble.

gargling and flossing with candy
*that helps, I*

*release the bunnies.*

combing through
*my do*
(and don't)
loosening
moose, rats, hare, and beehive
and any any
number of small would-land creatures, I

catch.

*when they do land*
business end up, wouldn't you know it,
right near my snarled ends...

# About the Author

Karen Robiscoe's stories, essays, & poetry have appeared in numerous literary journals, including *Spectrum* at UCSB, *Steam Ticket, Lunch Ticket at Antioch,* and many others. A resident of California, her byline: Fitness Front appears in several papers nationally.

Keep up with the author at
https://charronschatter.com

www.ingramcontent.com/pod-product-compliance
Lightning Source LLC
Chambersburg PA
CBHW071356090426
42738CB00012B/3139